Little Book of Answers

How Are Oceans and Lakes Alike?

Written by Ben Smith

Earth

Vital Vocabulary

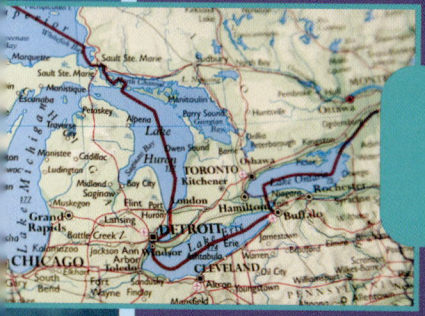

animals 12

lakes 6

oceans   4

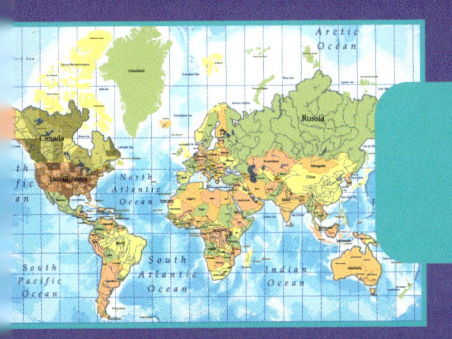

people   8

plants   10

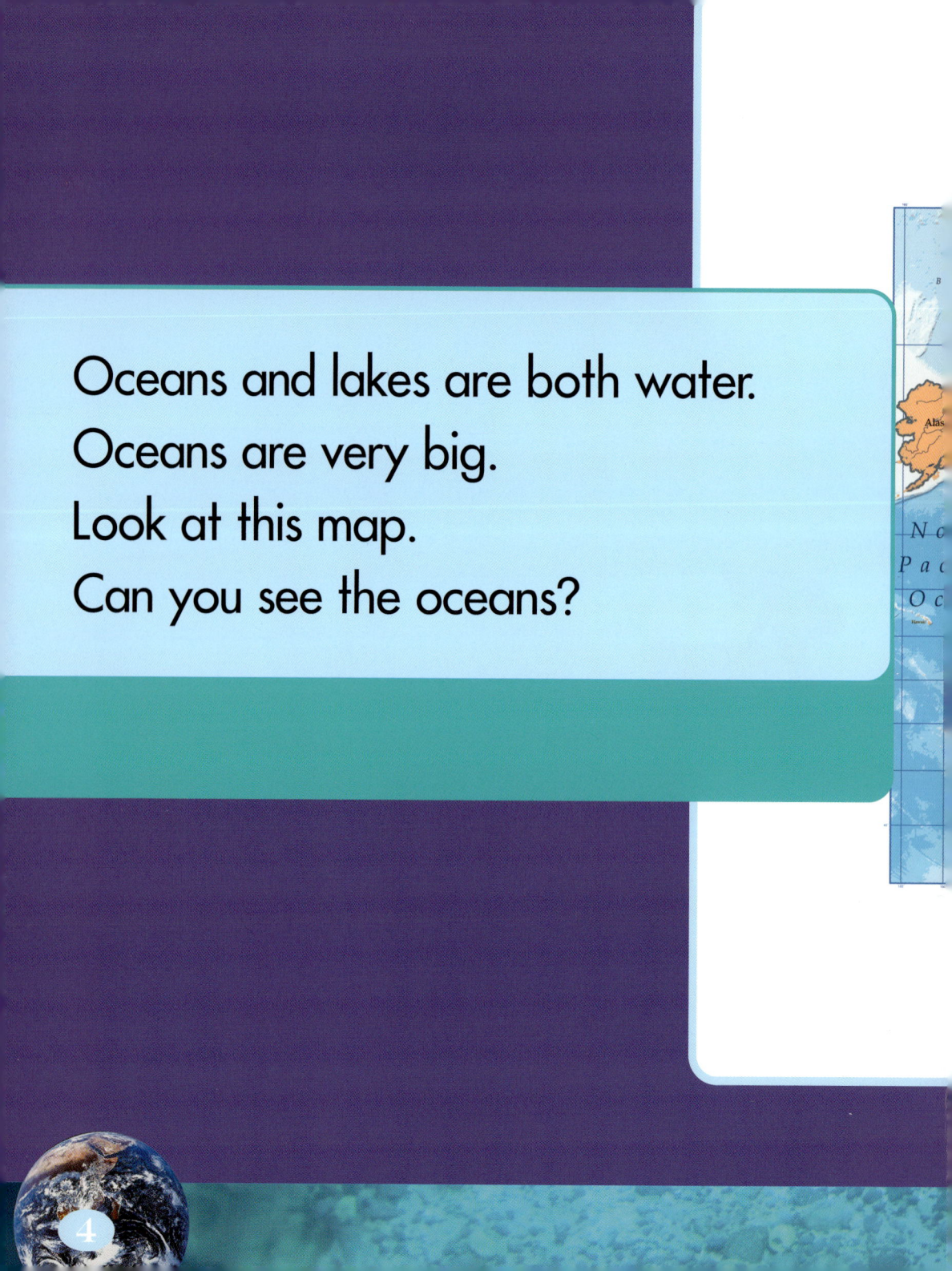

Oceans and lakes are both water.
Oceans are very big.
Look at this map.
Can you see the oceans?

Arctic Ocean

Atlantic Ocean

Pacific Ocean

Indian Ocean

The Pacific Ocean is the biggest ocean.

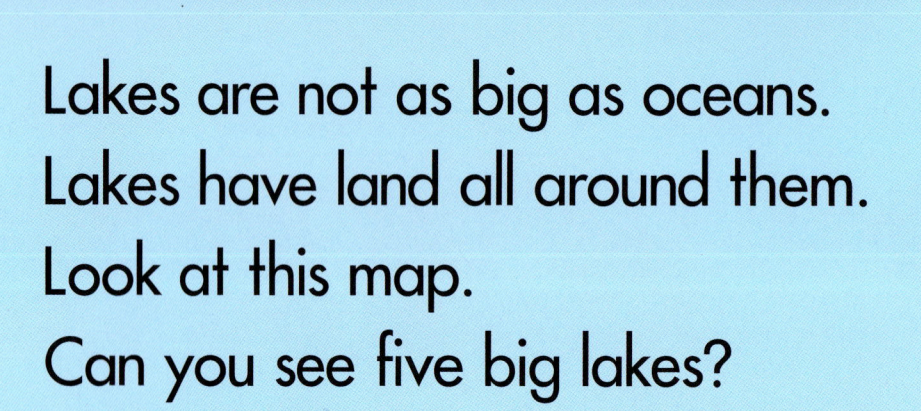

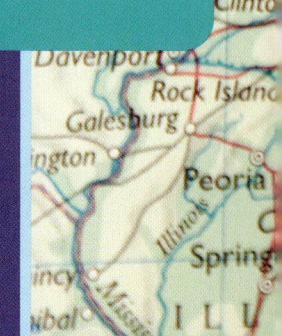

Lakes are not as big as oceans.
Lakes have land all around them.
Look at this map.
Can you see five big lakes?

The Great Lakes

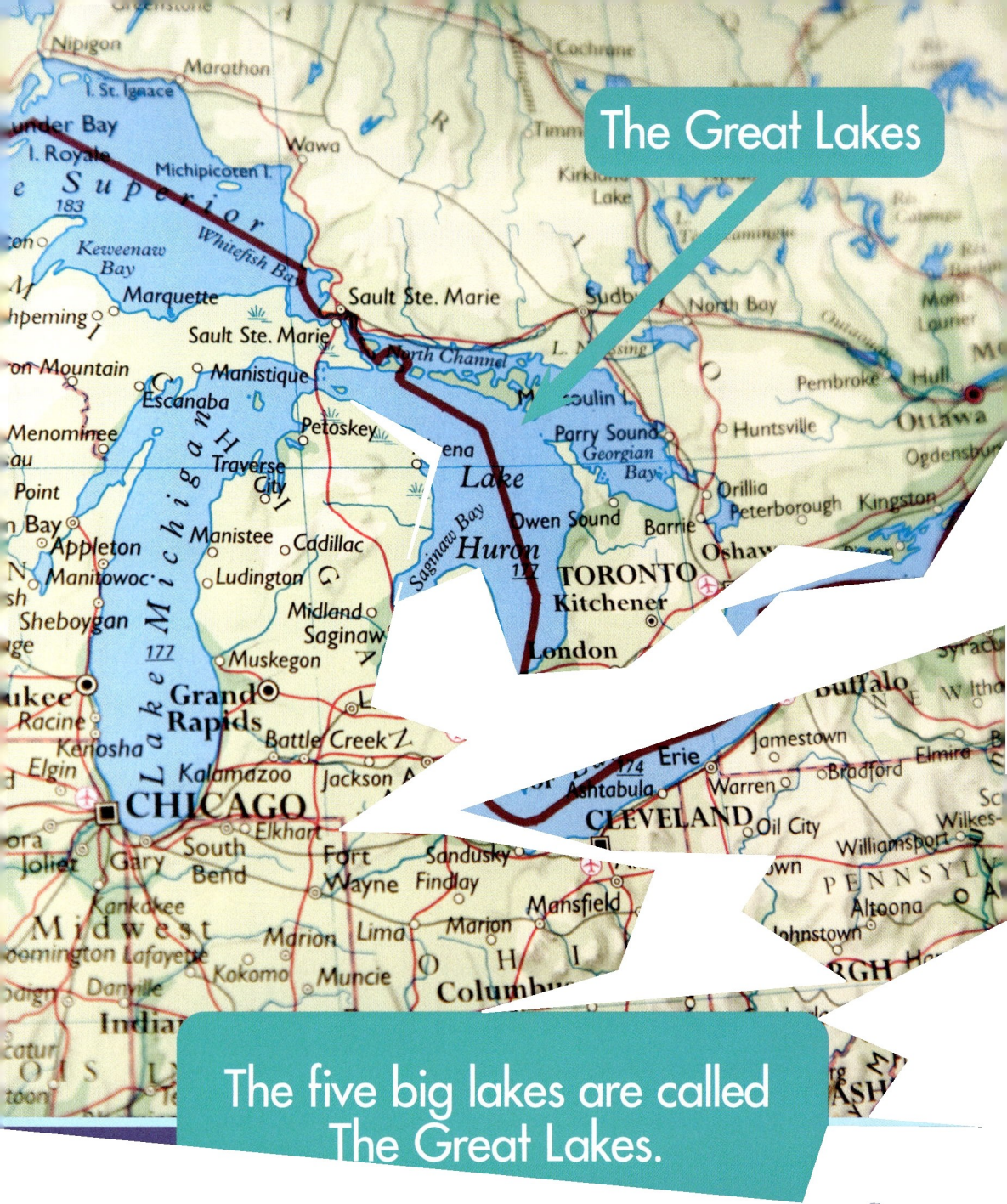

The five big lakes are called The Great Lakes.

People can play in oceans.
People can play in lakes.
They can surf in the ocean.
They can skate on a lake
if it freezes over.

frozen lake

This boy is surfing in an ocean.

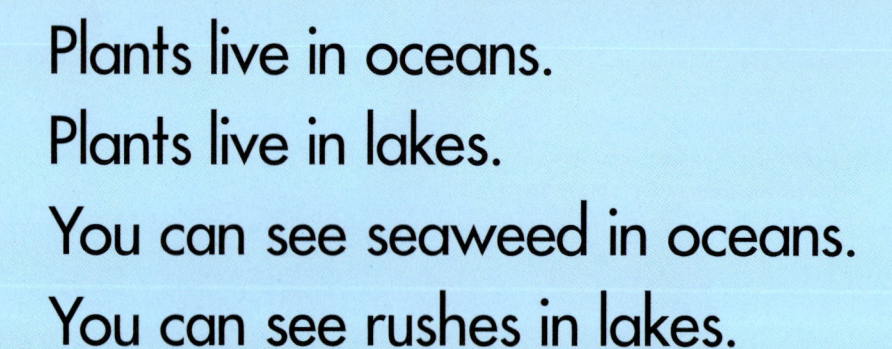

Plants live in oceans.
Plants live in lakes.
You can see seaweed in oceans.
You can see rushes in lakes.

rushes

You can see seaweed on the beach after a storm.

Animals live in oceans.
Animals live in lakes.
You can see dolphins in oceans.
You can see frogs in lakes.

frog

Dolpins jump up out of the ocean.

fish

turtle

You can see fish and turtles in oceans.
You can see fish and turtles in lakes.

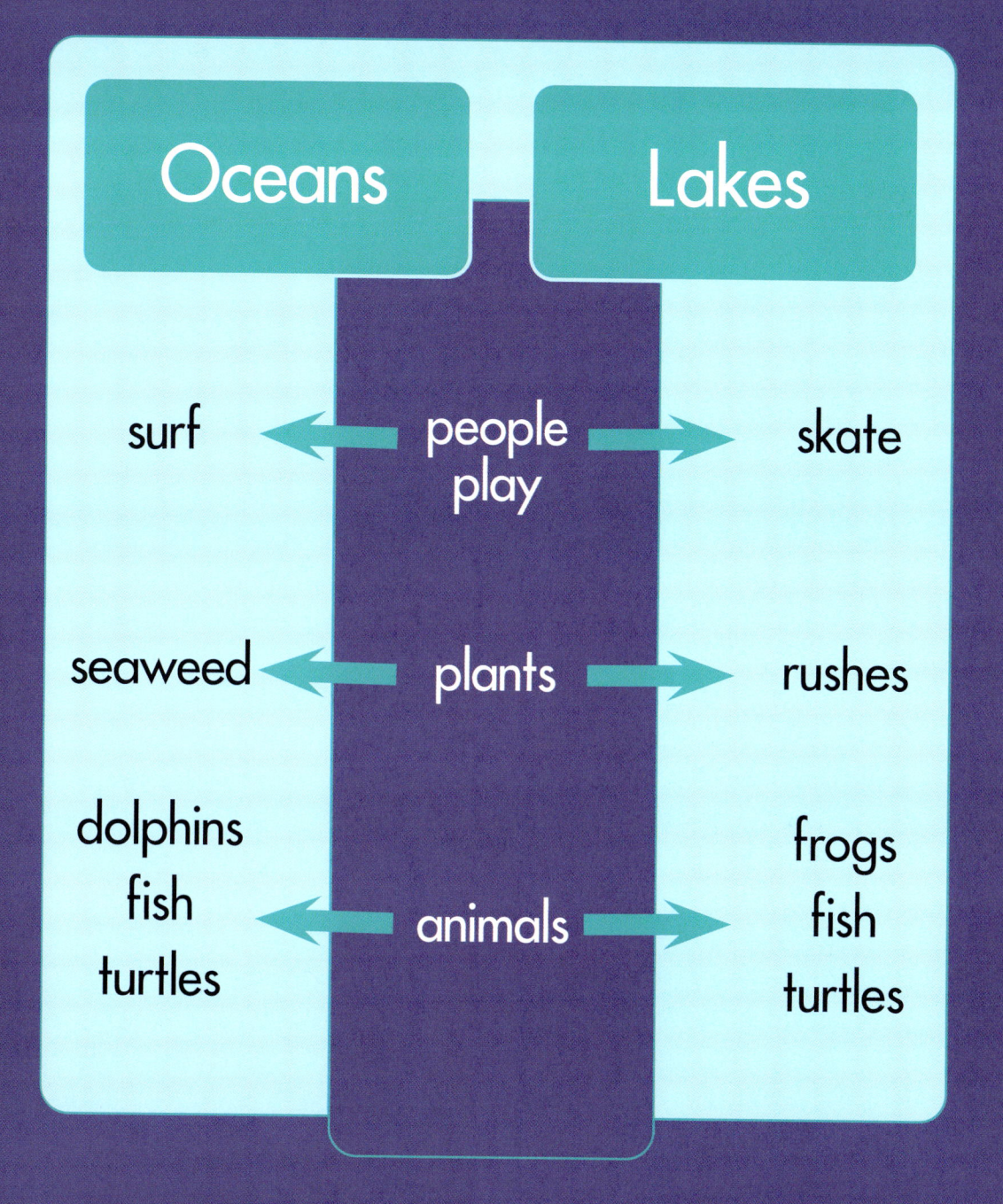

Oceans		Lakes
surf	← people play →	skate
seaweed	← plants →	rushes
dolphins fish turtles	← animals →	frogs fish turtles

Critical Thinking

Find out some other things you can do in both oceans and lakes. Start with these photos.